S0-BON-785

Time for Love

Assisted Living Viewed by One of the Very Old

Janet Carncross Chandler

Foreword by
Joanne M. Smallen, MSW

Papier-Mache Press
Watsonville, CA

Copyright © 1995 by Janet Carncross Chandler. Printed in the United States of America. All rights reserved including the right to reproduce this book or portions thereof in any form. For information contact Papier-Mache Press, 135 Aviation Way, #14, Watsonville, CA 95076.

00 99 98 97 96 95   5 4 3 2 1

ISBN: 0-918949-91-2 Softcover

Cover photograph © 1982 by Edith Royce Schade

Interior photographs by Edith Royce Schade

Cover design by Cynthia Heier

Interior design and text composition by Leslie Austin

Proofreading by Erin Lebacqz

Manufactured by Malloy Lithographing, Inc.

Library of Congress Cataloging-in-Publication Data

Chandler, Janet Carncross, 1910–1995
    Time for love: assisted living viewed by one of the very old / Janet Carncross Chandler.
        p.   cm.
    ISBN 0-918949-91-2 (acid-free paper)
    1. Aged women—United States—Poetry. 2. Congregate housing—United States—Poetry. 3. Aged, Writings of the, American.
I. Title.
PS3553.H27123T56   1996
811'54—dc20   95-43611
                                                          CIP

To Deborah,
    with gratitude to you for being
minister and friend to my mother, Mig Royce,
        with love,
            Duffy
        (Edith Royce Schade)
            January, 1996

As always,
to my loved husband, Bill, dead these eleven years;
as always, to our dear sons and their families.

To Sandra Martz and Shirley Coe,
without whom I'd be a lonely, largely unknown poet,
and whose gift for creating beautiful books is valued
by many poets, photographers, and story tellers,
most of us women.

To Joanne Smallen,
who wrote such a glowing Foreword.
My only regret is I am *not* a marathon runner,
never a runner at all, but a good fast walker
and a hardworking poet who loves her craft.
Now I mostly walk back and forth to the bathroom.

To my sisters and fellows in assisted living,
especially those who struggle for each breath. Also to
their relatives and care providers who do the best they are able.
May they succeed as well as my care home lady, Delores (Dee)
Page, who tries hard to give each of her six a comfortable home
with opportunity for creativity and affection.

To Bill Van Fleet,
who gave us five happy months before my progressive
far-advanced lung disease made such time together impossible.

Contents

Foreword

What a happy coincidence to be recruiting participants for my doctoral dissertation study at the same time Janet Carncross Chandler was completing *Time for Love!* My firm belief that those of us in gerontology need to be asking older people themselves about their experiences in long-term care was a strong impetus for this study. Better yet, Janet did not wait nor need to be asked. Rather, it is clear that her words sprang from her own inner imperative to express and share her thoughts and feelings about "living while assisted."

Having now read the entire manuscript of *Time for Love,* I can wholeheartedly recommend the poems and prose within. They are truly artistic expressions of extraordinary honesty and courage by an eighty-five-year-old woman with pulmonary fibrosis. As such, they can stand alone. However, I can also recommend this book as one that will help people who have a personal interest in long-term care because it affects them and their loved ones.

People like myself with parents who may need long-term care in the not-too-distant future have concerns about what this will mean for them and for us. Readers who have parents already living in a long-term care facility may be wondering how they can best participate in their parents' lives. Janet wrote openly about past and current relationships with her sons and their families, her deceased husband, Bill, and her recent friend, "Bill #2." She told what it was like to be old and need assistance while striving to maintain autonomy, dignity, relationships, a sense of humor, and, as she related in "Staying Alive Is Hard Work," life itself.

Readers who are already receiving long-term care may view these topics from another perspective. By daring to speak frankly about subjects that are frequently taboo in our society, Janet's words have the power to dispel loneliness for people left to wonder in silence whether anyone feels like they do.

In gerontological jargon, Janet's work also fulfills a pioneering function; that is, it illuminates the way for those of us who are not yet old. Most important in my opinion, Janet's poems and prose give hope—hope that we too can balance the physical decline and loss of later life with a flourish of creativity and productivity.

An overriding interest of mine in the productivity of people in old age stems from combining my two areas of professional interest: long-term care and older workers. While it may seem a mundane term to apply to an artist such as Janet, she was an older worker, her health condition rendering an artistic process a physical laboring as well. Her work has the capacity to disarm policy makers and others who would limit health and social services for the older population because they believe older persons are no longer productive.

Janet's beautifully crafted work underscores an important distinction frequently made by advocates of aging: older people as a group are not a problem, as concern with the demographic trend toward an increasing older population often infers. Older people may be people *with* a problem or problems, and like many younger people with problems, they have much to offer.

"As you grow older, grow bolder" is the caption on a greeting card produced by the Twin Cities Gray Panthers. On the front of this card is a sketch of an old woman with white hair, running in a marathon with grace and strength. I did not meet Janet in person, but in my mind's eye, fully aware of her precarious health condition, I saw her as this woman. I think you will, too.

JOANNE M. SMALLEN, MSW

Introduction

We who are old know that age is more than a disability. It is an intense and varied experience, almost beyond our capacity at times, but something to be carried high.   —Florida Scott-Maxwell

My first contact with Janet Chandler was in 1988. After reading *When I Am an Old Woman I Shall Wear Purple*, Janet wrote: "Because you are clearly someone who understands that older people are humans and so, are apt to fall in love, even sometimes irrationally, I decided I would like to offer my new poems to you." Thus began what would be, for me, one of the highlights of my adventures as an editor and publisher.

I published Janet's poems in a collection entitled *Flight of the Wild Goose*. What I soon discovered was Janet's incredible ability to relate to others, transcending the boundaries of age, gender, geography. Her admirers include many well-known poets: Meridel Le Sueur, Howard Nemerov, and Mark Doty. Some of her most ardent fans, however, come from unexpected sources: Kyle Hogg, a twenty-four-year-old rock music reviewer from Virginia who wrote, "Every once in a while, something unexpected will come along and kick me in the butt so hard I just have to jump and shout, 'Wow!'" Or my thirteen-year-old niece who adores Janet's writing and waits eagerly for each new collection. (We published *Why Flowers Bloom* in 1993.)

Janet wrote about things that are important to her readers: love, relationships, loss, growing old, from which we draw strength, courage, awareness. And for the many of us heading along the much-touted baby boomer march to old age, we draw inspiration. Here is a road map from a woman who understood and accepted the reality of diminished physical capacity, but who refused to allow that to translate to diminished intellectual and emotional capacity.

Her gift to us is multifaceted. She spoke not as an outside observer (the source of much of our information about aging), but from within the experience of the "very old." She viewed her domain with a professional discipline developed over thirty years of being a "helping professional." She was unrelenting in her drive to observe and record her experiences. And perhaps most importantly, she had a poetic voice that lets us see the world through her eyes—to hear, taste, feel what it is to grow old.

When Janet began work on this book, she was "looking for a place to die." In an early introduction Janet explained, "For five years, following the death of my husband, I lived in a senior residence. When my pulmonary fibrosis reached the far-advanced stage, my doctor recommended a skilled nursing facility. It sounded like a place to die. My doctor told me that yes, this could happen any time—or not for years."

She moved first to one skilled nursing facility and then to another, attentive to how each place uniquely approached the care of its residents. In spite of the availability of twenty-four-hour care, her health and her will to live began to deteriorate. After three months, one of her sons offered to look for a residential care home near he and his wife and daughter, where Janet could have a warmer, more family-like environment. Within weeks of moving to Page Care Home, Janet's outlook changed dramatically. She began daily walks, continued her writing, and was able to resume attending services with her fellow Unitarian Universalists. And as Janet was able once again to extend herself to others, love and friendship flowed back to her. Her writing flourished and culminated in *Time for Love,* a moving narrative of her experiences with long-term care. Only days away from sending this new book to press, we received word from Janet's family that she had contracted pneumonia and died. Already she is sorely missed.

It is easy to consider Janet as the exception. But as Patrick Grizzell of the Sacramento Poetry Center once observed, "She is able to find in the simplest thing a galaxy of possibilities, and in the most difficult moment, a purpose. What she shows us in her poems is that it is remarkable that anyone is *not* these things."

Perhaps it is that we *do not always listen.* My hope for this book is that it will remind us how foolish it is when we do not hear, and heed, the remarkable voices of our elders.

SANDRA HALDEMAN MARTZ

Time for Love

Assisted Living Viewed by One of the Very Old

So Now I Know the Name of My Enemy

You who have AIDS
cancer or leukemia,
remember the day
you learned your diagnosis?
Before, you were barely conscious
of the word. Now it is everywhere.
It is in you and of you.
It has changed
you into someone else.

The day it happened to me
my wise, kind young doctor
moved closer.
"You and I have seen that you
are winding down—right?
Now we know why. You have a disease
for which there is now no known cure.
Pulmonary fibrosis—it means
over the years, bits of infection
have turned more and more
of your lung tissue into fibrous tissue.
Lung tissue is what enables you to breathe.
Fibrous tissue can't breathe."
He paused, watching my color, my pulse
observed that I still can breathe.
I said nothing, taking it in.

"So gradually, your shortness of breath
will prove fatal. Yet you may live for years.
Die of something else maybe. No one knows.

And during the time of your need for me,
I will be here for you."

I felt sorry for this new person
who had just received a bit of bad news.
But that was not all.

"I think you should go
to a skilled nursing facility."

When to Use Durable Power of Attorney

Twenty years ago at least
my husband gave me two split-leaf
philodendrons, complete with a huge rock
on which perched a snowy egret
all set off by a glistening
and fragile glass goblet.

Like me, the split-leaf parents felt a need
to nurture   grew one child after another
until their giant kin trailed after
all about my small apartment.
Last week I noticed a fetid odor
as of dying roots in a brackish pond.

Water had gathered at the top, no longer
nourished the plants. I scooped up the excess,
hoped the trouble was only my inattentive
watering.   Alas! My plants
had simply lived too long. Last night
I dismantled the whole, carefully

eliminating dead roots.   I cut off ends
of my twin split-leaves, poked them into water.
By morning   one had grown a single white root.
A few leaves tried to raise tired heads.

The other plant had been dead for some time.
No sign of renewed life. Why this heavy fatalistic
feeling, as I separate parents from offspring
then from each other   toss the dead plant
replant the one remaining?
One day soon   I am convinced
a brackish odor   no tiny hopeful root.
Time then for my durable power of attorney.

No Wonder

My subconscious
kept letting words like
death or dying
creep into my conscious self
or burst in like a bullet
so my poet-self
could not refuse it.
No wonder I kept writing
one death-poem after another
even though no editor
would take them
and poet-friends shuddered,
"Not another! Why do you
write those things, anyhow?
Please! Write something cheerful!"

My subconscious knew
how tortured my lungs
had become, screaming for relief.
I, unaware of fibrous tissue,
thought my death-poems were only
what any reasonable person
would want to know
about the future—
enemy all of us are sure to face,
mouth tight closed
against revealing
when.

A Day in the Darks and Lights of My Dying

7:00 A.M.

A bad day. Noticeably weaker. The little Chinese-American woman comes at seven to get my breakfast. She is a year my senior but still drives. Bent on keeping busy to avoid boredom, she helps other residents at our senior apartment far less sturdy than she. At the same time, she earns money to contribute to her church. She pads about in bedroom slippers, so as not to wake me until all is done. How much she reminds me of the nurse's aides that were at Bill's hospital in China. They resisted all my attempts to help care for my husband. "My job! Keep out of my job!" they demanded.

Noon

This is the first time I've found myself gasping for breath lying in bed. A shock! Even by lunchtime, I could barely creep around to fix carrots, soy yogurt, rice milk, and rice toast. Stabbing pain almost like heart attack, or what I imagine is that. Gone now, I am up and about.

6:00 P.M.

Probably my stabbing pain was anxiety. Nothing to feel anxious about, except that I'm slowly dying. Or fast. Was it only two days ago, my doctor suggested I go to a skilled nursing facility? At least there'd be someone around if it happened during the night.

7:30 P.M.

David and Dan and I had last three-way conference. I leveled with them. "I feel ready to die. Hope it's soon. Since I seem to be going this way, why not go while my mind's still intact?" I stress I'll only be trying to get comfortable, *not* to get better. "So don't feel sorry for me," I said in a rusty, lugubrious voice.

"We know you have to die sometime," said David. "If this should be your time, it's a good thing you feel at peace about it."
"You can't expect us not to feel sad," Dan said. I could imagine his chin jutting a bit.
"For a while, because you miss me. Not sad for me." I wonder how people without children manage.

Welcome

Everything but a band out to greet me when a friend's husband drives me over to be admitted. Both the director of nursing and the director of the entire six floors are out to greet me. Their smiling faces tell me I'm welcome and an honored guest. They explain again how the place is laid out—those needing no extra care on first two floors, those who welcome a little extra help on next three floors (called personal care). The sixth floor for people like me who need a skilled nursing facility. The young activities director wheels me up the ramp. Only two weeks ago I could walk up this ramp. Today, being wheeled feels mighty good.

Arriving at my room, shared with a ninety-seven-year-old woman, I am introduced to the nurse's aide who will be with me all the first week. A quiet young woman, friendly but professional, she exudes confidence. The towel rack and closet and, of course, my bed all know my name. These are important when I am afraid I may lose my identity.

Who will I be now that I'm here? That is the question.

What a Blow!

My doctor and I were finishing up his first visit after I had been admitted to my new home. It was a gloomy visit, filled with unknowns since my lung disease can speed along or poke, never know. I yearned for speed, as he well knew. No use taking forever about something that was inevitable.

We talked about my blue armband that designated me as one who would get no CPR if found unconscious. That seemed almost cheering to me. At least I'd not be kept on forever (or as close as could be managed) by tubes and medicines or surgery. What use when life had dwindled to mere existence? Just before he left, I wanted reassurance that what was left of me would go to a medical school so young medics could learn from my complexity of ailments. My doctor shook his head. "Afraid they, er . . . ," he hesitated.

"You mean they wouldn't want someone my age?"

He nodded.

"How about any part of me?"

He shook his head. "Afraid most of your systems are almost worn out."

Too bad. Even in death, they seem to prefer the young. I never thought there'd be a penalty for dying when you're old. "Well," I added, "at least I can have an autopsy."

"Only if you want to pay for it. You don't have anything rare enough to interest science!"

We had a good laugh together.

Chosen

For six years, my roommate
had reigned supreme in this room.
Most of that time, her
roommate was a good friend.
After she left, a succession
of short-term tenants. And now
another! I am convinced
that her determination
to really make it this time
was related as much to not wanting
to get used to a poet's foibles
as to feeling her ninety-seven years
was enough. When I asked her how
long she'd been here, her dour reply:
"Too long!" Then her Irish whimsy
turned this into a joke: "Before you
complain too much, remember, the more
complaints He hears, the longer God
lets you live."

After hours of tortured breathing,
her attentive nephew and his wife,
who knew the symptoms, asked
the local pastor to give her
the last rites. In an aside to me
he said that she had had
last rites at least five times before.
"I feel fairly sure she'll come through
again this time," he said, "but it
makes her feel we care to have it done."

Sure enough, she thanked her priest,
turned over, and went to sleep. "We might
as well go home," said the nephew.

All the next day, she demanded cold water.
And when night came, she wanted no blankets,
not even a sheet. "Window open! Wider! Wider!
More air! I can't breathe!" I felt sure she wanted
to know her spirit could escape
through the open window. So, even though
I chattered with the cold and a brisk wind,
I remembered her complaints story, and made none.

In the morning, she did not respond, had turned
away from the light. That spirit, so sturdy
for so long, wafted lightly through our open window.
Her mouth had a slight smile.
The Lord had chosen her!

Getting Used to a Bib

At mealtime, you might think
you were in a kindergarten,
everyone decked out in bibs
all along the hall
and in the dining room.
We could choose where we ate.
I liked that and promptly chose
to eat in my room.
There I assumed I would *not*
wear a bib.
How wrong I was.

I ignored it the first day or two.
After I had spilled chocolate pudding
on my next-to-best T-shirt, I decided
to try this pink-, blue-, and white-striped
bib, made just my size.
Little did I know of the joys
of bib wearing! Stick the ends
together around your neck with Velcro,
place a gaily colored paper napkin
straight down the front for protection
of the protector, and you can eat spaghetti
drink coffee or soup with perfect safety.
What if it did make me look
like an oversize infant?
At least I wouldn't be
an old lady with a spotted front.

You Never Know Who You'll Meet

As I got on the elevator this morning
a woman got on at the floor below.

She looked blankly at me. I knew that look.
Vague, not quite centered, somewhere else.
I wondered where she was off to alone.

At first floor, she gazed vacantly around.
"Where do you get off?" I asked conversationally.

"I don't know. Should I? Do you?"
"I'm seeing a friend, going out to a meeting.
Why not ask the receptionist to call your floor?"

She moved slowly toward the office, whispered
something to the receptionist, turned toward me.

The receptionist smiled, in that way they have.
"We know her well. She tells me *you're*
the one who doesn't know where you're going!"

Picnic at Fort Sutter

Our young activities director
tossed her long gold-tinted hair
about, as she does when she has
something fun to suggest.
"How'd you like a picnic tomorrow?"

Eight of us turned up,
seven in wheelchairs, I with my walker.
The lucky staff that shepherded us
and carried special food in neat brown bags
and linen for the tables, acted as if
we were their honored guests
(which in a way we were).
"You guys pay my paycheck."
We sat in the sun while
the staff served. Some of us talked
to each other. Three ate quickly and apart
from everyone else, immersed, no doubt,
in memories of other picnics, younger times.
We watched young people not watching us
or trying not to. We felt good in the warmth
of the sun, surrounded by tall trees,
church bells, and the adobe of Sutter's fort.

When we got home, two who had sat apart
almost smiled at me. One went all the way—
grabbed my hand and stroked it. "We had
a good time at our picnic, didn't we?
We're still a part of the world."

Reality Is Hard to Face Up To

"Richie!" calls my roommate, a bit more urgently than usual. "Where *are* you, Richie?"

I come to the rescue, though I know it will help only briefly. "Richie and his wife were here yesterday," I tell her. "Remember, they come Mondays and Fridays. Today is Saturday."

"But I want him to get me *out* of this place! I can't stay here forever."

I lock eyes with her. "Remember when Richie and his wife were here, they urged you to eat, so you could move back to your nice apartment."

"But I don't *like* to eat. Only once in a while when I'm *really* hungry."

I move away a bit. My roommate has been known to lash out at nurses for telling her she'd never get better without drinking and eating. She turns her gaze inward. *"Richie!"* she calls. "Where *are* you, Richie?"

Hey, Babe, I Have to Go to the Bathroom

My over-ninety roomie yelled at 3:00 A.M.

Babe was more often my name now,
my real name having disappeared as soon
as mentioned. Lady, Lady Jane, and rarely,
Kitten were other possibilities. It took
me a while to even think she might mean me,
especially in the middle of the night.

"Push your call button!" I told her,
with only a touch of the asperity I felt.
"Taking you to the bathroom is beyond me
and certainly beyond the bounds
of what a roomie should do. Just push!"

"What did you say? I have trouble hearing you."

I repeated my instruction in what could be called a yell.

She fumbled about, finally located the button.
"They'll never come. They act as if
I shouldn't ever have to go."

Exorcist

My roommate is complaining
about how she can't
say a thing, but
the one she's talking to
looks at her as if
she's "some kind of a nut."
The trouble is, her nurse
had simply been trying
to explain something to her.

Reminds me of a time when
I was having a telephone reach-out
with my psychologist son.
I'd been telling him about when
I was eight or so and I tried to swim
a quarter of a mile, accompanied
by my father in a rowboat.
Throughout my life, I'd hung on to
a guilty feeling that maybe
I'd touched bottom once
maybe even twice
which was *not*
in accordance with my father's
guidelines. I never
mentioned my uncertainty
to him, nor did he rebuke me.
So there it lay, the unearned dollar
I'd cheated to get, heavy
as a metal band around my head.

"Maybe I ought to do an exorcism
on that guilt," my son suggested.
"Now I've put on my official robe.
I place my hand about your forehead
and—abracadabra onesietwosie.
There. Guilt all gone!"

To my amazement, it *was* gone
never to return
until my roommate's
thinking nobody likes her
brought it all back.
Too bad I can't loan out my exorcist!

First Word–Second Word

First Word–Second Word is a word game I thought might help patient-residents living at a skilled nursing facility. My friend Mary's mother lived there. Often, she didn't speak much, not even to Mary. Other times, words bubbled out, but in a voice so soft few could understand. Mary was eager to have her try the game. It goes like this: After we've gone around the room, told everyone our name, the leader starts by saying the *first word* that pops into her head. No fair letting one part of you persuade you not to say your word (no good, nobody will like it, on and on). Just blurt it out. Person sitting on your right does the same. And so on around the room. Now we have a tiny poem, like beads we could string about our necks. They don't mean much yet, but it's fun to watch as Mary writes them on a big paper sheet.

Now for the *second word*. We go around again, starting with the same person. She relates to her word, however she wants. She might explain what other words came to her right after the first word. Or maybe she's lost the feel of the thud that word made as it slid out of her mouth. So she starts off on something else entirely. However each chooses. Simply say another word or two or three, add it to your first, and see what we have when we've gone all around the room again. Mary or I then read out all the words just as if they were a poem—which they are.

You can find your own words on the sheet of paper. Or maybe they've left you, and the words all look like someone else's. Either way it gets people liking the feel of brain telling tongue what to say and then seeing it come out on that sheet of paper. "Mine!" some feel but do not always say.

Little did I know, when we started this game, that soon I'd be one of you.

Seeing Right through Me

Today, I was out visiting patient-residents,
You Are Invited to Our "First Word"
notes in hand, taking in the eager looks.

"You have a letter for *me?*"
asks a neighbor down the hall
holding out her hand.
After examining it closely
she asked, as if it were a cone
with no ice cream, "Where's the envelope?
There isn't any envelope."

"I'm sorry," I told her. "I don't
have enough envelopes for everyone. And
of course I'd have to give one
to each person if I gave you one."
I was glad I remembered that if one twin
got something, the other twin did, too.
But this didn't help her much.
She nodded, but clearly would have preferred
a cone *with* ice cream.

Another neighbor down the row of eager, frozen,
or indifferent faces thrust a demanding
hand at me. "Where's mine?" She quickly shoves
the invitation back at me. "Read it, then.
You wanted me to have it. I guess you needed
some work, didn't have enough to do, so you
dreamed this up for yourself! So read it!"

The demanding hand grabbed it back from me,
then slapped it at me again. I took
the invitation, trying hard not to get embroiled,
stunned by how she
had seen right through me.
"Let me know if you change your mind," I told her.
"I don't care about your made-up work," she called
as I went on down the line. "Why should I care?
I'm not the one who needs work."

Roomies

The best way to define *roomies*
is by saying what they are not.
Roomies are *not* members of your family.
Nor are they friends—at least not at first.
Certainly not business associates:
teachers, ministers, legal advisors.
Not nurses, doctors, or psychologists
though you're getting warmer.
They are more like the persons
that share a room at a hospital.
You're separated by a drape
and are cared for by doctors and nurses.
But unlike the two persons in a hospital,
who may stay only a few days,
roomies in a skilled nursing facility tend to be together
for weeks, months, even years. Long-term care!

That is, unless one or both (more often, relatives)
complain that the other is intrusive, not
sufficiently aware of the other's need for privacy
or that the room's space is divided unfairly.
Relatives may demand an immediate move.
Sometimes all this is accomplished
without your knowledge
and within a day's time.

The one complained about may be unaware
of what is going on until she
finds a new roomie, a stranger, in the place
of her old roomie. All then is
repeated—the newness and strangeness,
mutual reticence to share intimacies
they finally got used to
with that person on the other side
of the drapes
so some lucky roomies had the feeling
of finally having a true friend.
After so rude a separation, who
would have the courage to try it again?

So before your relatives—or your roomies—
complain to the director of nursing
or send an alarum to the ombudsman, I hope
you will urge them to talk things over
first with you, then your roomie
and her family (if she has family
members who visit). Time enough then
to think of a room change for one of you.
Avoid, if you can, the trauma of being uprooted.

Gremlins Are Comin'

Those mischief-makers, the gremlins—
small gnomes who love to make things
balk or fall apart—are particularly
prone to Monday arrival here.

During the night, the bathroom light
goes out. No maintenance man until morning.
On my every-two-hour forays, I fear
for my life as I head toward the toilet.

By morning, the gremlins have settled in
for a productive day. The water stops dead
in the shower as my shampoo whips up a lather.
Not content with mechanical busywork, gremlins

whisper in aides' ears, "Why not call in sick?"
They do so in droves. Replacements are rushed
from the registry, need help getting started.
This is the moment the director of nursing

learns that the bigwigs who visited last week
will be back today to see recommended changes.
Who knows what the gremlins will whisper
in their critical ears?

Back in a Minute

Is a phrase you'll hear a lot
from nurse's aides
who have to juggle one patient's
needs against the other nine or ten,
whose call for help is apt
to come just when she's almost
through mopping up #610B.

This reminds me of earlier days
when our twin sons often
needed help in eating, bathing,
or toileting at the same
exact time. I too always *meant*
to make it back in a minute,
maybe less. But it didn't often happen.

Remembering how long my "minutes"
were helps me be more tolerant
now that I'm on the waiting end.

New Regulations

All of a sudden
everybody—nurses and aides,
maintenance people, even visitors—
pause at our doors, knock
or say, "Knock knock."

"What's going on?" I asked.
"All this formality!"

"New regulations," explained
the aide. "The people
who have been evaluating our program
want us to make sure our patients
are able to die in dignity."

It occurred to me some of us
might not think dying was what
we were here for. Of course
I didn't say that out loud.

"This is the only home I have left,"
my roomie mourned.

"Me too," I agreed. "So we have
to make out the best way we can."

"This is your home away from home,"
added our aide in her wry way.
"Less home. More cost."

The Undifferentiated *"Help!"*

First time I heard that *"Help!"*
it wailed through dark corridors
epitome of sadness and loss.
It came again, more faint this time.
Someone who has just arrived, like me,
I thought, and wondered if I should join
that ancient crone voice.

Next night, the *"Help!"* was followed
by a plaintive, "Where am I?"
Still something I could identify
with. A place where mostly older people live
where bedtime arrives soon after eight.

The first hours slipped by in a heavy sleep.
The rest of the night, a horror.
How had I ever landed here?
How long must I stay
in this place where only a few
seem lucid, most stashed away
by families worn thin
from wife, husband, mother, or father
who lost a little more
each day—same questions
never hearing the answers?

Inevitably, the final question
floated dismally through the night—
"Who am I?"

Oh, Night!

Oh, Night!
So young, so fair
such twinkly stars
promising the world
when one is young
and life looms sweetly ahead.

Oh, Night!
So dark, so dank
so filled with bad smells
hurt and pain
when one is old—
and winding down.

Oh, Night!
Mother, father, grandma, grandpa,
baby brother, older sister,
and my husband—all, all
took their leave at night
in the solemn and fearsome night.

Weighing a Welcome Invitation

My sons and I stay in touch
twice a week by telephone. Keeps all of us
abreast of what's going on. And me
from slipping into one of my depressions.

We'd gradually assumed I would continue
where I was until my final departure.
When problems loomed, they could be handled
by following Ma Bell's advice.

"I know you planned not to move again,"
one son told me. "But you might want to consider
our finding a place near one of us, or take turns
every six months or a year."

This sort of change had been ruled out
as I got older—and older. The idea
it was still possible—and that each son
was willing to undertake that extra
time, patience, and caring—
touched and warmed me.

Then I weighed the gains and losses—
new doctors, new places and faces—
against present-known troubles,
well-worn friends, town where I've lived
since my husband departed.
I have almost decided anyone
eighty-four best stay put. But, oh!
How I love being invited!
And that no one has to plan for me!

A Woman's Privilege

Was it only yesterday
I wrote about almost deciding
to stay put, since I was
too old to make such a radical
change? Well! Women have been known
to change their minds, regardless
of their age. And so I have.

When I talked with each son
by phone today, I quite suddenly knew
this is exactly what I want
to move close to one of them,
my near-living son, see him and his family
often enough to feel I am a part
of a family group once more.
It might not work, and then I'll have
to retrace my steps. But I know now,
for sure, I want to try it.

Surely my depressed times will be less
often and less severe when I am
and *feel* closer to one family and,
through twice-a-week phone calls
and occasional visits from
my far-living son, I'll seem close
to them, too.

My lungs suddenly fill with fresh air!

Page in Not Quite a Poke

Moving from one city to another to live in a new residential care home without having seen the place or the people is a scary business. That's what I did, with help from Dan and his wife, Betty, and daughter, Sasha, all involved in visiting the possibilities and sending me a list. One stood out. I knew this was *it*.

I telephoned. Delores Page, who runs Page's Care with husband, Tom, was quick, asked a lot of questions, answered mine with precision and good humor. It was her high-pitched laugh that made me feel we'd get along. Friends helped me pack, and Dan took my belongings by U-Haul. I flew in the tiny plane to Arcata. An hour later, and there we were.

And there she was waiting for me. We looked each other over. Apparently she saw how much I needed her kind of giving. I saw someone I could like. On the way to Page's Care, she told me about my new family. She and Tom, her "backup man," and Linda, who will keep our clothes clean, our rooms tidy, and in general, make us comfortable. Four days a week, granddaughter Sara, two, will be there while her mom works. Coalie, their black cat, completes the family portrait. I'll soon meet my five sister care-mates. To be continued . . .

Transplanted

Here I am
intact
uprooted
by my own choice
(and Dan and family's invitation)
huffing a bit more
but definitely
here   alive   floating
until strength returns
enabling me
to swim again.

Acquiring a New Mother at Eighty-Four

I never would have thought I'd need or want or even tolerate another mother. That was before I moved here and met Delores, who mothers all six of us. She takes a day or two to decide what kind of beastie each new resident is, then starts right in to create bonds that have her "ladies" staying for years. She does this with an individualized blend of hugs and subtle blandishments, fresh fruits and vegetables, treats each day, the kind of planned regimen kids need but will not always accept.

Struck by polio at eight, Delores was expected to die but survived a year in an iron lung. Nobody would know now of those years of torture except for her slight left-leg limp.

Polio seems the reason Delores turned to nursing, decided to share her skills and love with those who needed them, helping them concentrate on what they have left, not what they've lost. After eighteen years as head nurse in a convalescent hospital, she and her husband bought a plot of land and built a new home, just right as a residential home.

Six years later, she and Tom, with help from Linda (who fixes breakfast and lunch, sings out bingo numbers Saturdays and Tuesdays), run a home I'm glad to call my own. My time in the skilled nursing facility seems years distant.

Sara

Blue eyes wide
snack box firmly in hand
this almost-two-year-old toddles about
room to room
making friends
discovering
who has candy
which one welcomes a visit
anytime,
warming the hearts
of six older women
yearning for relationships.
Welcome small Sara, you help
to make this home
a family.

Six of Us

After learning names of nurses for three shifts, a different weekend crew, and one from the registry when a regular called in
sick, you'd think it would be child's play to learn five names at
my new care home. But a week after I moved in, I still grope for
Leticia and Gertrude, get Harriet mixed up with Ione. As to
Thelma, erase her—homesick, she persuaded a visiting son to let
her go home, though she couldn't be sure where her room was
after being here a month. So now we are five.

Each is polite, knows Delores and Tom, hopes I'll like it and
stay. But clearly it's hard to move over. Especially since I hadn't
even visited before I moved in. *What if I can't stand her?* I can
feel them say to themselves.

Gertrude spends even longer at crosswords than I at writing.
A thirty-year expert, she keeps three games going at once.
Leticia, nearly blind, fast going deaf, now in a wheelchair, un-
able to paint or play bridge any more, is curt when I blunder
and ask her about reading. "You forget, I can't see." Whenever I
turn to Harriet, she smiles blandly. "I don't remember. Doesn't
really matter to me." Ione, tall like my Aunt Ruth, has white
curly hair. Her head bobs rhythmically to inner music, takes life
as it comes. "You can get used to anything," is her favorite
phrase, adding she has lost two husbands and her only son. She
has a sweet smile. I gather she feels I'll mellow in time.

The one thing I find hard to get used to is the rule of silence
at meals. Nothing written, but eyes are on our plates. Delores, of
Portuguese descent and a super cook, prepares exactly what each
likes best or what's within her diet. Used to at least some give-
and-take, I flail about trying to find common ground. One
answers briefly. Others keep eyes on plate.

Today, I finally find the reason. "The food's too good to let
it go cold. Besides, we've lived together for years. Plenty of time

to talk when we feel like it." Take it or leave it, sister, they imply. Resigned by now to convent living, I find virtue in brooking no interference with my meals. When another prospect presents herself, I think I'll tell her what's going on—and why.

What You Should Know after Two Weeks

Only two things matter. With any luck at all, you'll know whether you like those who run the place. And can you and your housemates tolerate each other?

I don't think of Delores as a caretaker, so unobtrusively does she do little individual things to pleasure each one of us. The first day, she learned I'm a banana addict. One appears magically on my bedside table every night. I asked where I could get a spotted scarf cleaned. She de-spotted it herself. No charge. My walker seemed too heavy for one so frail. She "just happened to have" a lighter one. Every night and often during the day, she "knock knocks," brings a tidbit or a hug, suggests a food-choosing trip together.

Tom hangs our pictures, makes flowers and us bloom. Delores and Tom are less caretakers than friends.

As to my housemates. At first not sure of me, less so when it was apparent I did not share their love of bingo and Lawrence Welk on Sundays, they now seem to feel that, strange beastie though I am—with my poem-making and watercolors, only NPR and PBS for news and music—still, I'm human.

Today, Delores drove all of us around to see the sights. Clearly, we've decided to accept each other.

Getting Un-used to a Bib

It never occurred to me
there would be any problem
about getting unused
to a bib. Clearly,
I would not want to wear one
in my care home, since
others do not do so, might
consider me gauche. But how
to prevent that spotted-lady
look?

Not to worry.
Why else do we get pushed
close to our dining table?
I haven't sat up so straight
in many a year. And only
one warning spot.

To My Astonishment

I seem to be getting better.
Only four months ago
I entered a skilled nursing facility convinced
I would never leave it alive
and might leave soon.
When I came to my new care home
just three weeks ago today
I thought, "My, what a lovely
home. Too bad I won't be around
too long to enjoy it."

Yet for the last three days
I have clearly felt good
on awakening, maybe not
quite the first time
(I wake and wash at six, then
run back to bed for another snooze),
but by the time I have actually
gotten out of my snug nest
I can tell, though it seems
years since I've felt this way,
I feel good! Alive!

I find myself
looking forward, even though
each day is much like another.
Few events planned, I am learning
to take more and more pleasure
in little things.
How the purple hydrangeas outside
my blown glass window reflect
the same hues in my blue vase.
How I'm hungry for breakfast.
How much I like it that our care lady
comes in every night for a hug.
How my at-first-silent housemates laugh
as they teach me bingo, that dumb game.

How We Are A-Changing!

When I first came here,
I might have told you my housemates
were quiet people, inclined
to keep too much to themselves.

No doubt they might have felt
(though surely not said)
I was too extroverted, too quick
to ask questions, not wait
to let answers unfold.

Now I am converted to their way
of eating in silence, saying little
unless somebody brings up a subject,
not interrupting anyone's reveries.
Not to say I always keep to this.

Maybe, after living here a few years
I'll join them in patiently answering
a newcomer's Newcomer Questions,
hoping she'll soon wait for answers
not rouse us from whatever

thoughts we still have. And when the newcomer
slows up, listening more than asking, we'll
kid them a bit, let them know we are humans, not dummies
even if some still play bingo, that dumb game.

Lemmings Following the Piper

We six can be sitting quietly
in the "ladies" living room
in our big overstuffed chairs
each in her own seat (if you don't
believe it, try sitting in one)
letting our thoughts rumble
and bumble around our brains
as people often do before breakfast
while they wait for it to arrive
when Lisa calls out, "Okeydokey"
meaning breakfast is ready—
let's see, Thursday, so
it will be poached egg
(hot cereal, cold cereal
are Tuesday and Wednesday)—
and all of us start out
at what for us is a gallop
each in her particular order.
If one is slow or still
brushing her teeth, nobody waits.
The piper calls!

Dinnertime, the tradition
is repeated, with two variations—
the dinner smells have been
growing increasingly tempting
and our maître d' is Tom.
The very second he has served each one
he comes in, waves his silencer
toward the TV, announces, "Dinnertime!"

Before he gets the word out
we are almost at our seats.
Whatever TV program was on is forgotten.
Nothing keeps us from following
our dinnertime piper.

A Different Kind of Separation

Beginning with our departure
from our first cozy nest, through
the joy and sorrow babies feel
as breast is found and lost

and real food never quite takes
its place, losing, finding next level of growth

until the lucky find a lifetime mate.
And so for a time, there are only
smaller losses, as our children repeat
our patterns. A never-ending round of repetitions.

Now comes the hard part, the one
we've talked about and practiced but

never really thought would come,
not to us; others, maybe.
And when it finds us after all, takes one
or the other, rarely both at once as we

had fantasized would be the best, we duck
our head to shield us from the blow.

After a while, we realize we are still alive
might as well act that way.
And so we pick ourselves up, take time
to discover who we are, now one, not part of two.

Off we go to make a new life, one
that need please only us.

Months pass. Years. Suddenly, it seems
we must be growing older.
We walk and talk and think more slowly
don't hear or see as well. Daily, we test

whether memory too is departing—
the horror of that disease, what's its name?—

is always with us. Calamity strikes
once more. Heart or lungs or gut or all
give out, and we're off to a hospital, then
on to a skilled nursing facility

which either keeps us for the rest of our days
or spews us out as slightly improved.

Suddenly, we need more than living alone, afraid
we won't be able to manage, this time may break
an arm or leg, or fracture a fragile hip. More
than anything, we yearn for closeness. Friendships

are good but not enough. A blessed son or daughter
offers to find a place close by, to see us

often, at least once a week. Gratefully, we may accept
and if lucky, find ourselves in a care home only

a few miles from our rescuer. He carries out
his part of the bargain but at some cost

to him, his family, music, and job. This reminds me
of my live-in grandma, when she felt she might

be burdensome to my mother, took to her bed
and stayed upstairs. Not long after, she took off
for good. Her good. My mother's release. Our sadness
mixed with regret—and relief. No upstairs here.

I can immerse myself in poetry (as long as words
come out and mean what I tell them to mean).

I ask my two sons to call only when they're free and want
to keep in touch. I mean it. Crisis of moving is over.
Consciously, this time, I am separating myself
from all I hold dear—but cannot keep. One last separation.

I wonder if my grandma knew what she was doing
when she moved upstairs?

Even Paradise Has Flaws

Until now, three months
since Dee picked me up at the airport
introduced me to my new home,
I've thought I'd tumbled into paradise.

Dee's mother taught her to run
a clean house, have clean things to wear
and plenty of nutritious food. So
that is what she provides for us,
the six under her care.
She wants us to enjoy a comfortable nest.

True, it takes a while to get used
to thinking of how what I do will affect
the other five. I was so sure my TV and radio
could be kept low enough, but after
trying it a few weeks, I gave in, got
headphones like the rest.

I still remember my mother's horror
when I used a slice or two of onion
in a casserole. Onion was verboten
in my family's home. And as to garlic!
No garlic ever sullied our kitchen.
Dee relies on both for gourmet taste.

But the day paradise flaunted its flaw
my doctor recommended I go to a specialist
two towns from us. I was all ready
to make an appointment when Dee ruled out
driving that far. "We have an eye doctor
just as good right here." The flaw began

to rumble underneath my feet. An earthquake?
No. Only a simple fact of life. She couldn't
be away from the others that long. I knew
my son would drive me if it were essential
but I couldn't expect it otherwise.
How about my going by bus?

Dee vetoed that. "You're still not strong
enough," she ruled. I remembered needing naps
even when I'd only gone for my walk.
I thought about it overnight, then decided
paradise had to have some boundaries.

Appraisal

Almost three-and-a-half months to the day since I moved from Sacramento to McKinleyville and started my new life in a care home. Could I make that big a jump? And even more important, could Dan and his wife Betty, daughter Sasha, move over a bit so I could feel a part of their family group?

As far as I'm concerned, I give a rousing *Yes!* to each. Living in a place where I feel at home, close to my son and family but not so close I'll be intrusive—perfect! And Dan has made sure we see each other at least once a week. I've experienced a demonstration of ethnic instruments (including Dan's new lyre) put on by his musical group, attended a recital in which Sasha played her violin (superbly) and an art show of children's work, listened and munched at a posh art auction in support of California's health proposition—Dan and his Big Foot Family Band played—went to a campaign fund-raiser for a county supervisor candidate. Sometimes we share meals, sometimes not, as with any extended family.

And David has been my faithful telephone communicant, every Wednesday and Sunday at quarter of eight. He's freed me to go back over that period when my husband lay dying, so I could find any lingering feelings of regret or guilt that might have contributed to depression. Two weeks from now, he and son, William, will cross the country for a weekend visit.

I've felt closer to both sons and their families than in years, yet don't have to worry—as I surely would if I lived with one or the other—whether it might not be creating tension. My new life has been a blessing to me.

Trade Off

I sleep as long as I want
ten hours, wasn't it?
If I feel like it, I make my bed.
If not, our all-purpose helper
is glad to take over.
Breakfast is served just before 9:00.
After, stop off at bathroom, one of two
for six older women, then I'm free
for the day, with no plan in sight.

Let's see, shall I catch that fleeting poem
I almost tagged last night? No. Gone.
Oh, well. Maybe tomorrow. Another if not
that one. Read Harriet Doerr's new book?
Call about that workshop in Eureka?
Register for upcoming election?
Write more of those blasted Change
of Address forms? Stop for lunch.
Time for a nap. Discover other half a banana.
Nice day for my usual walk. Let's see
if I can make four blocks today without
huffing too much. Another nap on return.
Possibly a letter or two or a few postcards.
Then dinner. Sure to be delicious.

Too bad my five tablemates are so dedicated
to eating while food's hot. Or too
familiar with what each will say
that nobody says anything until all
have finished, then we give out sparsely.
By 7:30 all six doors are closed for the night.
I'll read this week's *New Yorker*, shower,
fall asleep easily.

Appreciating the Appreciators

Today, first time I've met people
of good will who want to visit old folks
living in a care home.

It was something of a jolt
to think of myself
as a recipient of community concern.

After all, I pay my way,
twice as much as I did
when living in a one-bedroom
senior apartment.

Then I remember that both older and younger
folks need to be in touch with each other.
I'm glad to see this group of girls
all in grades four through six.

Their leader, grandmother of the young group
leader; eager to know us, want
to share their songs in return for our
telling them about our lives. Fair enough.

So we sketch out where we came from, why here,
where our families are. They don't quite
ask what church we go to, but a particular
faith is mentioned several times.

They have sweet young voices, sing out
like fledglings practicing individual warbles.
"Popcorn in the Apricot Tree" is their favorite.
Then the leader finds out I'm a poet.

Suddenly, I'm free to share my dearest friend
my only real talent, with children who may
one day be poets too. I read about the network
of friends I discovered after my husband died.

They listen quietly, nodding as I stop, make sure
they see the simile between the brown branch
turning green again, and myself, still alive
after all, somewhat to my surprise.

Only a few know about a chrysalis. But they do
know about butterflies. And they like the idea
of a butterfly, sad, yes, and angry to be shrouded
finding out it's been growing wings all along.

The grandma leader shares that she, too, is a poet.
So is one of the girls, tall, sober looking—
like me at her age. We agree we'll meet again
exchange talents and help each other.

How chagrined I was for my errant thought
they'd come because we might be poor!
Their gifts were of the spirit.

Color Dancing on My Windowsill

Beyond our picket fence
and row of trees on nearest mountain
sun has painted sky
a faint pink-into-apricot.
My collection of blown glass
begins to share its beauty.

First time I've had so wide a windowsill!
Glass needs sun to bloom.

When I wake on a sunny morning
my prize, a coral vase I bought for one-fourth
its price because the maker considered
one minuscule nick marred it, shines out
at me, lighting up fruits indolently
leaning on one another. The mere hint
of a dancing figure. Flower of gold leaves.
And in the corner, three coral-into-red stars.

One day I went on a vase splurge, bought soft blue
decorated by blue notes; two with hues of roses:
frosted pink cross-hatched in bronze and gold,
and clear, deep rose with bursts of autumn flowers
turning into gold as sun strikes them alive.

Each of my sons gave me a vase, taller by half
than all the rest. David sent a clear dome within
an even larger dome, dominant, quiet about it.
Dan's gift is tall as David's but shaped and slender.
Hold it one way and a scalloped form appears,
turn it about a trifle and a myriad of patterns.
These come and go, never the same.

Accent points: a black chunk of onyx
reflects and plays with whatever is mirrored
in its smooth surface. My purple vest and prison-
stripe T-shirt play games as I move in and out.
A geode, pebble exterior belied by bitter-chocolate
interior, four-cornered black star and white core.
Gifts I would never have except for a friend.
Swedish glass in egg shape, with four balloons
and four times four bubbles forever playing together.
Deep blue, almost purple striped tiny bowl, just right
for holding small stones which take turns sitting atop
Dan's weathered, highly polished driftwood.

When I take in my treasures, all my past
returns to me, color on color, with sun predominant.

Bingo, That Not-So-Dumb Game

Now that I am a regular—play
bingo *en familia* with my home mates
twice a week, Tuesdays and Saturdays
at two—I view it with a less jaundiced eye
can see some virtues which were not
evident to me before I played.

For instance, it keeps us alive to the
day of the week, how close to next bingo day.
And when it comes, there is an alertness
about each of us, a willingness to take
a short extra nap. If someone is sleepy,
she may slow things up by fiddling
with her store of change, always an irritation
to others, who do not say anything (bad form!)
but make their faces look as if they're tapping
their feet with impatience. Then, too, we want
to take in at a glance if we have 30, 40, or none
on our board as well as the highest
and lowest number for each B-I-N-G-O row.
That way you save energy and might call out that
glorious challenge one second faster than
the one who is just taking in her good fortune,
has not yet checked to make sure it is true.

What a joy to congratulate the winner!
Not many winners in our lives these days. And if
it should be you, enjoy! Next time it will be another.
Finally, we have the pleasure of volunteering, we
who thought our volunteer days were over. Linda, our
all-around helper, scurries about on bingo days even
faster than usual, so one of us folds towels for her,
another sets out our equipment ahead of time.

Bingo reminds us the world is built from both
cooperation *and* competition, and it's OK to crow
a bit when you win, even if we all know luck
is the only thing that really counts.

Preventive Visit from van Gogh

Usually, my preventive dreams
are reasonably oblique,
maybe the end of a long hall
leading to a room decked out in white
or a feast not ever quite
in reach, lots of available liquids.
This time, van Gogh paid me a visit.
He carried a gleaming, newly sharpened
knife. I wondered if he meant to cut off
his other ear, but did not ask.
With a flourish he brandished his knife
(by then a dagger, maybe a sword)
over *my* right ear. "Can't you hear?
Time to seek relief, my dear.
Else I surely shall cut off your ear."
I dragged myself reluctantly out of bed
to do away with his threat, and found
he was indeed right.

Winter Solstice

Winter is a time for joy and singing, sledding, jolly times. But winter too is a gathering up of feelings left over from spring. Not every hopeful tulip pushed, opened, and flourished. Summer feeling of long, sere days when tempers flared, relationships wavered and turned sour. And fall, when bright leaves presaged early first snow and a hard winter ahead. People find themselves obsessed by looking at the obituary column, especially if they're over seventy-five. Then we remember the Hemlock Society and Dr. Kevorkian. Why should we suffer when it's clearly our time to go? Indeed, who would miss us?

Each one will want to make his or her own assessment. I could not end my life knowing the ones I love would grieve and in a different way from simply mourning my loss. *If she can't stand her burdens, when she has so many blessings,* they might very well say yet not express, *how does she expect us to do it?* Those with kin may not have that bolster. In the end, it has to be you who finds someone, some thing that reminds you the world hasn't always been so dun colored and may not be again, if only for an occasional joyous moment. For me, as I was musing about this poem— between spells of coughing and coughing and getting only sticky stuff quite capable of clogging my diminished airways—I looked in our bathroom mirror and stopped coughing to watch the strange dance going on beneath the skin below my eyes. I have often wondered about this dance, sedate or wild, how it lets me know my heart, nerves, bones, even my misbehaving lungs and gut are still gyrating about in my body—this dance tells me, *I am alive.* I can feel and love and make choices. If I had stopped that dance last year, think of all I would have missed!

Visit from Robin

Young woman singer-composer from my church.
Powerful full-blown voice.
Songs from her heart, she told us.
Long straight hair. Black.
Hazel eyes.
Body to match that voice.

Invited to visit
she came bringing Zachary, six months
and still connected to his mother.
First we exchanged her tape of songs
one of my books of poems.
She thumbed through, lingered
over the poems about nature.

Then we talked about her remarkable voice.
Even as a young child she took
deep breaths from way down.
"Life   love   courage   kindness, I'd say
as I took a breath in.
Fear   anger   hate   rage
as I let them go, harmless used-air puffs.
Use whatever words you choose."

I could feel her taking in
my breath, shallow
as a child's wading pool.

Gnidilskcab

It doesn't take much—
a few amber drops
escaped before I reached
my destination—
can spell incontinence
to one in a panic.

Too much energy
expended from too scant a pool
can require a day, two, three
before I dare venture
a walk around my care home.

My unstable stomach
passed on its complaints
to my already rebellious
ailing lungs—and I
was miserable for hours.

Today I'm down to one hour.
On poor days, could be fifteen
minutes when my body and lucidity
intermesh smoothly. But, oh,
what a beauty-filled brief time
that can be for one
on the way up again after
backsliding.

Spider Herder

My husband, Bill, still struggling
with what to do in retirement
after a year of thinking someone
would offer him another social work job
relapsed into boredom when it began
to seem this wouldn't happen.
When I started down the volunteer
route, he insisted he'd never do work
for free that he used to be paid for.
Then he discovered jumping spiders.
Soon he was absorbed in learning to take close-ups
of gorgeous eight-legged creatures decked out
in brilliant yellows and reds, rich browns.
"You haven't seen a spider until you see her
four eyes that look right through you
close up," he told our photographic friends,
who seemed unimpressed. "Just hiding
their fear of spiders," he told me
and added, "How'd you like to be my spider herder?
I should say arachnid herder, I guess."

Now I had just discovered poem-making and hoped
herding would not take all my time. I wondered
vaguely whether spiders bite, and are their bites fatal?
Bill spent happy hours learning the formula
for close-ups. Buying the proper flash
equipment and a new close-up lens took more time.
He scouted our yard, especially the ivy along
our stone wall, looking for likely subjects.

For a time, he was deflected by a common garden spider
named argiope, a large, spectacular beauty
with gold and brown horizontal stripes. A skilled web maker.
Not a jumper, so my services were not needed.
I could see that eventually, quite soon maybe,
I'd have to give herding a try. "Just place her
right here," he told me. "I have both my flashes set right
where they should be if she's precisely there.
All you have to do is keep her there."

I started out with a pencil, coaxing a wary
and quite tiny spider onto the surface,
only to have her jump off the second
I tried to place her on her spot.
"Why not use your finger?" Bill suggested.
I didn't like to have him find out I was scared
near-witless lest I be fatally bitten. I waited
until he gave me the signal: "All set. Ready, wife!"
Ah! He knew I needed bucking up, that was clear.
Gently, I picked up the spider with my right hand
placed her on my left thumb for stability.
To my amazement, she made no move to jump off.
But when I unloaded her, off she swung, and no
amount of effort brought her back into view.
Bill was disappointed but not discouraged. He
gave me a warm husbandly hug and went off
to find our next subject.

About the fourth spider, I discovered
one who learned or intuited that if she simply stood
still for a moment, maybe two, she would not
go through the torture of being retrieved and replaced.
Soon I found that all jumpers shared this trait.

Only one ever bit me. It was a tiny bite,
more a warning nip than a real predatory nibble.
And I had kept her going rather longer than most.
One of the results of my herding was Bill's
immediate jump into Camera Club fame, where
he was given the title of "Our Spider Man."
We spent wonderful close hours together
sharing his absorption, his joy in finding
something beautiful instead of a dull life.

Bill has been gone these ten years. No spiders to herd,
I find my absorption in poetry. I still miss
those years together. Last night, when Bill came
to visit and exchange a word or two, he
raised his right eyebrow as he used to do,
called me fondly, "My little spider herder!"

Two Fiddlesticks

Past the circle of whirling dancers
she runs, afraid she may be late
for Fiddlesticks, the name she
and her father chose for their
Norwegian folk music duet.
Their turn next.
Dan's eyes meet hers. "Not late—
just ready for us."

She handles her violin as if it were
a part of her. Together, the tall
father and ten-year-old daughter
consult about their A strings.
Important they be in tune
with one another.

I hear a ripple of amazement
go the rounds of the dancers.
Surely this young girl
will never keep pace
with their flying feet.
Members of her father's musical
group know better. Sasha is a professional.

Sasha's mother, Betty, arrives.
We flash proud smiles at each other.
The light shines on Sasha's rosy knit.
Golden hair cascades down her back in waves.

The dancers get set, and are off with
the first mingled fiddle sounds.
A kind of skipping step, embroidered
by twirls and fancy Norwegian steps.

As I watch these two, both so loved
by so many, so intertwined in their music
I remember you, Sasha, the second day of your life
close to your mother, your father and his big smile.
I remember the year your father stayed home
to have his experience in caring for you—
day after day you played games or you painted
in your backyard. Once a week, I visited
and we went to the library or park. How I treasure
memories of those days!

Thank you for moving over
when I came up here to live
so again I can be an extended part
of your family. Happy birthday, Sasha!

Staying Alive Is Hard Work

Almost as hard as it was wondering when I would die.
Since my first family doctor thought I was "winding down"
advised me to do whatever I needed to go in peace,
I saw Death right around every corner.
For almost two years!
Of course he, and later doctors, usually used
that loophole: "You have a good heart—you *could* live
for years."

Switching to a more hopeful outlook means I must
learn to ignore my pain each time I try to breathe,
persuade my lungs to keep on, praise that good heart,
cajole my body into eating whether or not
it likes what's sitting expectantly on my plate.
Like any Grand Canyon mule, my poor old systems
yearn to be permitted to turn back, lie down. Those
mules know all too well what's ahead.

Today NPR told of a prestigious man of ninety who just died
of lung trouble. How I wish he'd left me a message—
a way to survive those last five years.

Changing a Long-Held View

Means revising
not only what I say
but what I do.

My care lady suggests ordering
two Beconase, so I'll never
run out. No longer can I
put her off, "Who knows
whether I'll *need* two?"
Instead, I agree, "Good idea."

My families could be understandably tired
of my talking about *going*—
then never leaving.
Like a guest who has overstayed
her welcome. No family should
be in this kind of limp suspense.
A limit to all things!
I can imagine one of my grandkids
telling a playmate: "My grandma?
Oh, she's been dying for years!"

What I hope is to plan each day
so I care for myself, help those
I love and care for
maybe even someone worse off
than I.

Hugging Companions

First week

Late for church (UU, the kind that always sounds as if it's waiting just for you), I slipped in, sat next to you, nodded. You nodded back. Strangers, we exchanged a few words after the service. "Should think some kids might be scared, wouldn't you? So real!" You pointed out the joy of kids around us—loved the heroes, hated the villains. We exchanged names. I left. You left. *Finis,* I thought. As we approached the exit door you turned around, gave me a friendly hug, UU fashion, mentioning what everyone knows about hugs and apples. "If one's good, two's better," I said, as I gave you a hug back. You looked surprised but kept on hugging, blocking the way of smiling younger and luckier couples.

Second week

This time, I was early for church, sat down alone. Along you came. "May I sit next to my hugging companion?" Not *finis* after all! After the service you told me you were about to go off to Bali. Your son thought you needed time away to recover fully from an auto accident. Leaving in three days. "Too bad," I told you. "I'd give you one of my books to read on that long flight. But I don't have one here." So you came to my house. It took us an hour or so to discover we were within four years of one another, both had lost mates (your loss only seven months before), and we had grown children in their fifties. All the similarities that mean more with age. I showed you my husband's and my photographs, and of course, family pictures. Between subjects, we hugged.

You left. Off to Bali. Not quite. Two days later, you arrived with an artist's carrying case. A watercolor of a blue heron you'd done just for me. Two days after you left, two letters, one with a swatch of clippings about your exploits in long-distance running, honors in marathons. The last, you, your son, his son, and his son (the baby in his stroller) running as a family. Proceeds to go for Cancer Society, which named you Man of Courage for running while still under treatment for cancer. I was glad I'd told you about my pulmonary fibrosis. Two people lonely for closeness, skirting the age when closeness may no longer matter. As for now, hugging need not be a preamble. A therapy and pleasure on its own.

Bill from Bali Calling

First call
Like any sensible older woman
I was readying for bed
at nine-thirty
when you called and asked
if I had a man in my life???
"Yes," I replied. "Since last Sunday."
"Too bad. I thought I
might have a chance."
That was the way we started.
It was hard for you to understand, so
you did most of the talking. Bali
was as you had hoped—lush and green
and all colors. Beautiful people.
You and your son were having a fine time.
In fact, he thought he might give up
his job here and move there—at least
for six months. "Six months! That long!"
I tried not to let my voice betray
my disappointment (that you, too, might leave
for so long.) After all, we hardly
knew each other. And seven months ago
you were still a married man. Go slow,
I told myself, smiling as I remembered
my son Dan's advice: "Pretend you're
on a first date." But who our age can even
remember our first date—so long ago—
spouses and babies and teenagers
joy and loss and jobs in between
then and now.

Second call
You again started out kidding—
"Hard to carry on a courtship
from so far away." When I mentioned
I thought we were friends, you said
my poems made you feel you knew
me well. Your son liked them, too.
Ah! He's discovered the fastest way
to a poet's heart, I thought.
You and he were sitting on a wide verandah
watching a kingfisher, gorgeous bird
with unbelievable colors. Tomorrow you
and he will ride a motorbike
out to the rice paddies, he in front
you behind, hoping you won't hurt
your still tender leg.
All kinds of wildlife in the paddies.
Your son now seemed sure he wants
to fly home when you do, come back and stay
as long as he chooses. "Great having him
right here with me." And there also goes
my hugging companion, I thought.
Who could leave Bali after six months?

Now Is the Time for Love

"The time is short,"
sang a man's voice on NPR.
"Now is the time for love."

If not now, when?
In our early eighties—
would I ever find another
knight in shining armor
just waiting for someone
to respond to his hug?
Would you ever find a woman
so eager for your hug?

The ring of life is elusive.
Grab it we must
while it is still bright and shining.
And while it is still within
our reach.

News
March 11, 1995

Dear Sophie,
Thanks for your blow-by-blow
account of the poetry reading.
Clearly, everyone rallied to your plea
made up for missing members.
I knew you could do it!
Now! I have great news. A new man
in my life. Architect, painter,
also a UU. Many things in common.
Don't expect frequent letters.

Dear Annie,
I was in the middle of a letter
to you when Mary telephoned
so she got my news first.
By now you've probably heard.
Instead of an almost-eighty-five-
year-old, living a sedate life
in a care home, I have blossomed
into a young thing with a life ahead.
No matter how long—or short.
Wonderful what a new man friend can do!
He is a creative person with many interests.
He and his wife, both architects,
had a business together. Speaks well
of both of them. He's a painter of birds
and abstracts. I've been gifted

with a great blue heron on the search,
a Balinese jay, and a river li from
their trip to China. He likes my poems;
I like his painting. The liking has spread
to caring and all that can mean.

Dear Mary,
I'll bet you didn't expect
to hear such remarkable news Saturday
when you telephoned me—that I should
be lit by a new and bright flame
is beyond my belief, but not my longing.
It is all right to tell anyone who asks
how I am. You can say wonderful!
Thanks for phoning at the right moment.

Dear Harriette,
Thanks for your second letter.
You and others have waited
in vain for some word
that I am still here.
My neglect is due to a remarkable
man. We found each other in church!
He had just returned from the hospital
and the whole congregation cheered.
So of course, he went around hugging
his friends. Though we'd not met
I got one, too, promptly gave it back.
A hug multiplied can be pretty memorable.
We're having a splendid time getting
acquainted with each other
sharing assorted family and friends.

Dear Marion,
I can imagine you've guessed
when I stopped writing so abruptly—
she must be in love! No longer looking
for marriage. Much simpler to enjoy
being close to someone.
I am again learning to love.
Life is such an ephemeral thing—
best catch the ring as it flies past,
hang on while we're here.

Dear Suzy,
Sorry I've grown so silent.
Your fine letter gave me a jog.
I'm taking the easy way—
sending each of six friends
to whom I owe letters
a copy of a conglomerate.
Occasionally, in the midst
of my own joy and surprise
that Bill #2 has come into my life,
I think of each of you, fleetingly
wonder about this and that.
None of you has the pull
of my now-not-so-new
man friend.

Janet CC

PS: We just survived our first crisis!

First Crisis

Two months into the relationship
we began to have second,
third, even fourth thoughts.

You, eighty, lost your wife
not quite a year ago.
I lost my husband ten years ago.
Cancer almost bested you.
A car accident nearly finished you off.
My lungs have been turning
into fibrous tissue.
As you put it wryly, "Perhaps
we deserve each other."

From our first hug, a lively courtship
daily sharing of homemade soup,
family secrets, music.
Your painting and photography, my poetry.
Your awards and honors, my joy in my writing.

Always, the hug warmed us, two lonely
people, growing older together.
How both had yearned for the touch of another!
We swayed to "Scheherezade"
or James Galway's flute seduced us
with "Claire de Lune."

We progressed from home to movies
and plays, a first night together
at a Victorian B&B. Here the proprietor
bursting to know our marital status
assured us she didn't care
if we were a "clandestine couple."

So, too soon, we pondered
how it would be for me to share your home.
But not yet, not for at least a year
after your wife's death.
We wondered what fellow and sister
church members thought of our hand holding.
"Let's not flaunt it just yet,"
you said. Yet somehow,
word got out. People smiled
when they saw us drive off together
for an after-church tryst.

Too soon, alas, each began pondering
at our difference in stamina.
"How about a weekend in The City?"
you asked, when I often struggled
for breath to get up in the morning!

You had a slip of the tongue,
passed it off as a joke. "Will people
think I'm giving my Aunt Nellie a night out?"
That was a blow!

Yet a look in the mirror
made me see why you'd wonder.
If only I were five years,
better, ten years younger!

Serious reservations crept in
when you phoned an old family friend
assured her she was second on your list.
So this is where we are—in a crisis—
undone by slips of the tongue
my age and ailments,
your uncertainty
about yourself, now you're eighty.
So I am waiting
to talk it all over.
How to do it so neither is hurt in the process?
Egos intact, you could look for a younger—
or decide we are lucky.
I could return to acting my age
or we could work out ways
to love and to cherish
accept each as we are
imperfect.

Bill at Home

Some old redwood trees, beauties.
A crab apple in pink bloom.
Mini-orchard of apple trees, just budding.
Three months ago, when I first visited,
immense daffodils sprinkled new-green grass.

Bill parks his sporty Nissan
and with a one-two-three helps me
get out. Good days, I can do it alone.

Two large stones hold back the gate
invite me to walk down the boardwalk
leading to a rambling, welcoming house.

A glass door looks through to a wall of windows
indoor-outdoor continuance.
A wisteria shines, shimmers pale purple;
will get darker in summer, Bill, proud
homeowner, assures me. He and his wife,
both architects, designed this home together.

This is a home where art lives.
Each wall of the wide open living room
shows off Bill's birds, real and imagined,
vegetables growing below and above earth.
Bill's son—poet, B&B host, artist—
has an abstract, might be a Picasso.

His second daughter has a
conscious-unconscious painting; I see
it as a picture of family.
Make of it what you will!
First child is a psychiatrist.
Bill tells me about his family with pride.

His family reminds me of my sons.
Our assorted families are about the same age.
They lived through the turbulent sixties, opposed
the Vietnam War. Now all seem to be settled.

Bill brings in an apple blossom bouquet
for our table, chops fresh vegetables for the soup,
different each time I come. Clearly, he likes
creating his special foods after fifty-four years
of his wife doing the cooking. How we change with the years!

In this setting, I feel free to drift into intimacy.
We share secrets as we watch glowing embers.
We feel close and are growing more so.
Each hour together a pleasure.

Ultimatum

Don't bother to watch for me
anymore, Death.
I've given up peeking around corners,
setting out flares to attract you
expecting each moment
I'd find you soon
and get done with you.

Tonight, two weeks after my eighty-fifth birthday
that time I thought would surely be my end
if not before, I woke up suddenly
the way it used to happen
and wrote out a tame version
of my decision to change course entirely, head
for 2000 A.D. if not 2002, see if somehow, some way
I can outwit that pulmonary fibrosis
that's got me dangling
in a brisk wind;
see my grandkids
when they're well settled
in their professions
maybe even have found their mates;
maybe I can enjoy a few more caring hours
with Bill #2—why should we stop
at six months, just because he has cancer and
I this miserable beast that boils up gunk
and dares me to not spew it out?

Why should I not at least try
to share vicariously in the lives of my two sons,
surely the best sons any mother ever had.
Everyone will at least be glad to
not hear me talk and write about death—including me!

So, onward toward 2000! Live for the moment!
Untangle myself from the dangle, sly old Death's helper
has bound me round with. Head out, Janet!

Two Half-Moons

What would you think
if you wakened at 4:00 A.M.
and there
in a dark blue sky—
not one but two
half-moons?

The first half-moon
bright and glowing
smiles down at me benignly.
The second follows after
at a respectful distance—or
is the distance between them
a matter of mutual preference?
The second is pale, as if
not really
alive.

Then I remember.
That summer before
our fatal trip to China
you photographed the moon
late summer evenings while
I wandered about, picking bouquets
returning to give you encouraging hugs.
The sweet strains of "Claire de Lune"
drifted out through our French doors.

Now you are gone. Ten years.
Is it possible?
Once more I have found
a man with your name
someone who loves gardens
even your favorite song
who photographs friends instead
of the moon, solidly rooted
in staying alive, a man who
loves to touch and to hug
shows me he cares—and I
care about him.
You and I had fifty-two years.
He and I will be lucky
to have one.

Which one is the bright moon?
Which the pale one?
And why when I never
saw two half-moons before,
do I see them tonight?

Toting Up Gains and Losses

As always, I tend to teeter-totter
on a taut rope. You too.
We've so many loving and good
times to tote up!

Yet I still worry—will you
get safely home on a rainy night?
Sometimes you let me know.
Other times you get immersed—

who has phoned, what message.
You assume I'll know you made it.
Nearly every time you call for me
I'm almost ready. Big word, *almost!*

Forgot to take my stock of medicines,
dark glasses, my green hat, a toothbrush.
Even though you rarely complain
you'd have good reason.

So when you forget to buckle up
assure me you did remember on the way over
(as if *that* would make me feel better)
I realize this might be your way

of complaining about my not being ready.
One of these days, maybe we'll learn
to use words instead of acting out feelings.
Before our sum is upended by a rear-end crash.

A Fleeting Look

One of our serious conversations.
I had told you no man could take the place
of Bill #1, even though he died
more than a decade ago.
Not even you.
I watched the look on your face
as a passing light played upon it.
Incredulity?
Disbelief?
A touch of sadness?
Then a fleeting look—
a momentary gleam in your eye?

I and You and We

When you were married
to your spouse, I to mine
each couple worked out
our own ways of relating.

No spouses now, we
have to decide
whether the old ways—
ingrained after your fifty-four years
our fifty-two—are right
and feel good for each of us.

Mostly, we need to start from scratch.
I am no architect, not a
mathematical genius.
You are not a social worker
nor a recluse.

You and I can reach for our own "we"
while you still keep your newfound
joy of living more freely
and I struggle to squeeze breathing
and poetry in before our we.

Delight

Early in our relationship
when I asked my friend
how he made the home he'd just showed me
turn out to be such a delight,
he said he built delight of the eye and spirit
and a few other things right into it.

Delight is what Bill yearns for.
Marathon running was a delight
for almost twenty years,
collecting medals like finding
treasures on Shell Beach.
Helping his wife get through
her final illness a kind of delight.
Finding he could still bicycle
through lovely North Coast valleys
a delight, when running again
after a leg injury made this
seem improbable.
Not impossible, mind you.
Never say never to Bill.
Delight is what he aims for.

Morning Has Broken

My favorite hymn wakes me—
"Welcome the sunrise . . ."
A spreading glow of pink
against a bank of purple clouds
floods the eastern sky.

Outside our bedroom window
wisteria trails, peeking in.
Beyond, a young maple unfurling
a cherry tree in rose bloom.
Background of redwood.

I let my eyes and fingers revel
at finding Bill at my side, gently
touch his warm, still firm body
and marvel we are together
in his lovely home.

He's still asleep, surrounded
by cats. BB, black, sleek, sure
of his welcome. GG, still a kitten
challenges BB from blanket ambush, snuggles
against Bill, bounds about.

So far, Bill has never lost his temper
with me or the pets. That scares me a little.
He looks over to me, smiles, holds out
his arms. I move into them.
"Beautiful morning!"

Hugging the Sunrise

My new friend
tried his hand
at writing poems.
He wrote about feeling
so joyful he gave a hug
to the sunrise and sunset
and to every man, woman,
and child he met.

"That's fine," I told him.
"Only of course it's hard
to hug the sunrise."
I meant it as a joke.
But he took me seriously
took out the sunrise and sunset
and used day instead.

"It might be even harder
to hug a day," I joked.

All at once I remembered
the art teacher who didn't like
my lovely purple cow. "You *can't*
color a cow purple! Only brown
or black and white."
I did the cow over just as she wanted.
I even kept inside the lines. She was
great on line-keeping.
But I gave up art for many a year.

Oh, dear! I thought when I realized
I had done the same thing to my friend.

I hurried to my telephone.
"Please forgive me," I begged.
"Of *course* you can hug a sunrise.
Yes, and a sunset too
and everyone you meet.
When you feel joyful
you can do anything!"

First Poem
by Bill Van Fleet

It started with a joyous enveloping
hug that filled my body
with an inner light.

It has become a newfound weapon
against the ills of mankind:
old age, the blahs, the blues,
depression, and just plain pain.

As it works its wondrous way
into my psyche, I find myself
greeting each sunrise
each sunset
each man, woman, and child
with a hug full of warmth and affection.

To My Dear Friend and Promising Poet

Who would think I'd be jealous
of a new poet—one who,
twenty years behind me in experience,
already knows, having completed
his second poem,
it is better to show than to tell
(no need to say
Freshwater is picturesque,
you'd already described it),
a line may end where you choose.
Yes, and you know to respect your readers
let them find their own meanings
not insist on your own.
You already know poems need not rhyme
though a few rhyming words
almost hidden within a line are fine,
as your rosy rhododendron
hid its glory from casual observers.
I know you hated to give up
on long, intricate words. Use these
sparingly, partly to let your reader know
you know them, more because this is precisely
the word you need for that gaping hole
in the second stanza.

Some of these treasures I still
have trouble remembering!
No wonder, my dear Bill, I am not only
proud of you—also a tiny bit jealous.

Dear Bill

Remember that long row of windmills high on a cliff somewhere south on Route 395 or 5 or maybe 99, as you drive to or from the desert? How they plunge and leap and break stride then jitter and flitter another way, all in the space of a mere flick of time? Bill #1 and I, off for our annual trip to Death Valley, used to watch them and marvel that such changeable beasties could provide reliable electric power.

Since we met in January, that's what I've felt like—a windmill. No will of my own but pushed by a strong wind, ever since that night I so precipitously told you I wished I could move into your beckoning home. Lured by its openness and your welcome—daffodils, crab apple blossoms, warmth of your fire, your wonderful paintings of birds. BB and GG, your almost-Siamese cats: he large, sleek, black, dignified; she still a kitten who loves to torment him into a bat of his paw. She soon curled up around my neck.

And then there is your own private redwood grove. Remember the day we pushed our way through brambles to get there? How you held me and made my heart flutter?

Now, finally, this windmill is becalmed. Fickle winds may still push real windmills about. Not this one. I've made up my mind, plan to keep to it. My yearning for a home, for your home with you in it, is entirely beyond me. It isn't one thing. Not even three or four. All things point the way, for both of us. You, wise one, know this. Now I know it too.

Second Crisis
by Bill Van Fleet

I phoned at eight-thirty:

"Good morning, my dear Janet. It's a beautiful morning
over here. The cats are playing. Azaleas
are blooming, and the sun feels warm on my back.

"I could pick you up just before lunch—Progresso soup with
fresh vegetables and your favorite salad.

"After, I could read you a chapter from *Bridges of Madison
County.* Then we could take a nap under the redwood tree."

You replied:

"My dear Bill. I thought we had decided we wouldn't see each
other today. Both my sons think we should cut back our visits.
Seeing each other every day seems to sap my strength.

"Also, dear Bill. Maybe you should be looking for another,
a younger woman, more fully endowed, who has more energy
than an eighty-five-year-old."

"My dear Janet, before I broke my leg I was surrounded
by well-contoured young things who had energy to run
marathons. But the truth is

"I fell in love with you, who are aware of your 'sags and
wrinkles,' but you also wrote in that poem: 'let a new man
come into my life / and all my senses quiver. My eyes
take on rekindled spirit, my breasts perk up.'

"As a man, who could ask for more?
I am reminded of the name of a famous
apple grown in these parts—
    'Seek No Further'."

A Note in the Lonely Night
by Bill Van Fleet

Unopened Progresso soup in my cupboard.
Unlit candles in my bath.
Undisturbed side of my bed.
Untouched Kleenex box.
All bear silent witness to your absence.
BB, GG, and I wish you were here.
But we realize sadly you would be,
if you had the energy. Instead
of none to spare. The price
of a pleasant dream
might be gasping for midnight air.

One Last Toll Gate

We can be sure
there'll be an Exit sign
and one last toll
as we leave
this world of frequent pain and sorrow,
pay for our capacity for joy—in self
in family and friends
in mates and all children
in gardening, creative arts
little treasures;
and toward the end
a room of our own,
loved ones nearby or reaching out,
someone (or more) to bring us comfort,
and companions
in like circumstances.

Papier-Mache Press

At Papier-Mache Press, it is our goal to identify and successfully present important social issues through enduring works of beauty, grace, and strength. Through our work we hope to encourage empathy and respect among diverse communities, creating a bridge of understanding between the mainstream audience and those who might not otherwise be heard.

We appreciate you, our customer, and strive to earn your continued support. We also value the role of the bookseller in achieving our goals. We are especially grateful to the many independent booksellers whose presence ensures a continuing diversity of opinion, information, and literature in our communities. We encourage you to support these bookstores with your patronage.

We publish many fine books about women's experiences. We also produce lovely posters and T-shirts that complement our anthologies. Please ask your local bookstore which Papier-Mache items they carry. To receive our complete catalog, send your request to Papier-Mache Press, 135 Aviation Way, #14, Watsonville, CA 95076, or call us at 800-927-5913.

About the Author

JANET CARNCROSS CHANDLER, eighty-five, lived in a long-term care facility in northern California. Her husband, Bill, died in 1984. She was the mother of two, David and Dan, and the grandmother of two, William and Sasha. She was a social worker for thirty years prior to her retirement in 1971. She held an MFA in Writing from Goddard College (1988) and an MSW from the George Warren Brown School of Social Work, Washington University in St. Louis (1960). A poet for over twenty years, she self-published three chapbooks—*The Colors of a Marriage* (1982), *Poems for Poets and Other Fragile Humans* (1983), and *"How Are You" They Ask New Widow* (1985)—and *Significant Relationships* (1988). She also published *Flight of the Wild Goose* (Papier-Mache Press, 1989) and *Why Flowers Bloom* (Papier-Mache Press, 1993). Her poetry appeared in numerous poetry journals, and she authored three plays.

Ms. Chandler was an active member of the Unitarian Universalist Society of Sacramento (later belonging to the Humboldt Unitarian Fellowship) and the Older Women's League (OWL). She continued to write, having recently created a newsletter, *News, Views, and Reviews,* which she edited and published (and her son Dan composed on his computer) from her care home.

One of Ms. Chandler's objectives in sharing her experiences, was to remind us to take good care of our health. Having learned that lung diseases such as hers can be treated if caught early, she gently encourages us to seek medical attention at the earliest signs of illness. Ms. Chandler died November 1995.